My vocation is love!

By Love Alone

Enfolded in Love Series

Julian of Norwich: Enfolded in Love
Daily readings of love, forgiveness and joy

Julian of Norwich: In Love Enclosed
Daily readings of vision, compassion and hope

Thérèse of Lisieux: By Love Alone
*Daily readings of the 'Little Way' of love,
trust and surrender*

Teresa of Ávila: Living Water
Daily readings of poverty, union and mission

THÉRÈSE OF LISIEUX
By Love Alone
Daily readings of the
'Little Way' of love, trust and surrender

Introduced by Luke Penkett

Edited by Michael Hollings

DARTON·LONGMAN+TODD

First published in 1986 by
Darton, Longman and Todd Ltd
1 Spencer Court
140 – 142 Wandsworth High Street
London SW18 4JJ

Second edition published 2000
Third edition published 2004

This fourth edition published 2019

Arrangement © 1986, 2000, 2004, 2019 Michael Hollings

ISBN 978-0-232-53403-0

A catalogue record for this book is available from the British Library

Designed and produced by Judy Linard
Printed and bound in Great Britain by
Ashford Colour Press, Gosport

Contents

Preface	9
Introduction	11
Readings with St Thérèse of Lisieux	15
Bibliography	75
Index	77

Preface

The original *Enfolded in Love* series began some forty years ago with a selection of readings from Julian of Norwich's *Revelations of Divine Love* which sold more than 120,000 copies world-wide and is recognised today as an established classic, its teaching and presentation as fresh and enabling today as it was back in 1980.

This new series, with revised Introductions and up to date information, is published with a new as well as a returning readership in mind yet continues in a form that encourages us to engage with the great spiritual mentors through daily reading and meditation, allowing God to speak to each one of us and helping us not only to enrich our spiritual lives but also to survive in a world that presents us with hard and, at times, painful decisions to make each day.

Introduction

Marie Françoise Thérèse Martin was born into a profoundly devout family at Alençon, Normandy, on 2 January, 1873. At the age of five her family moved about 100 kilometres north to Lisieux and when she was only fifteen she entered the Carmelite monastery there and became a discalced (unshod) nun. Two of her natural sisters were already living there as nuns and soon her third sister joined them, again as a religious.

Sr Thérèse of the Child Jesus and the Holy Face – the name 'of the Child Jesus' was chosen for her when she received her habit; she herself added the name 'and the Holy Face' when she took the veil – passed away on 29 September, 1897, aged only twenty-four from tuberculosis.

The Carmel practice on the death of a religious sister is to circulate a brief biography of that sister to other Carmelite communities, or Carmels, and to ask for their prayers. In Thérèse's case, in spite of her early death, her spiritual autobiography *L'histoire d'une âme*, *The Story of a Soul*, written under the vow of obedience, was sent round in 1898 and had an immediate and amazing response, further copies of it being made, lent out, and read by non-Carmelites. The autobiography was published the following year. In just a little over a quarter of a century the work was known throughout the Christian world. In 1925 Thérèse was canonized by Pope Pius XI. In 1997 she was named as a Doctor of the Church by Pope St John Paul II, the youngest person ever to be so named.

As a nun, Thérèse was remarkable for her simplicity. A couple of months or so before her death, she told Mother Agnes, her natural sister, 'I feel my mission is to begin soon, my mission to teach souls my little way.' When asked what this 'little way', *'la petite voie'*, consisted of, Thérèse replied, 'It is the way of spiritual childhood, the way of trust and absolute surrender.' It was to be her sister Pauline, however, who introduced the phrase 'the little way of spiritual childhood'; Thérèse uses the phrase only three times in her writings. This was a short, direct, and new way of being, free of all complexities, full of hope, and confidence, and love. It is quite astonishing how her teaching has spoken to so many people from all walks of life.

Thérèse became known as The Little Flower of Jesus, or simply, The Little Flower. in May 1887. She had approached her 63-year-old father, Louis, as he sat in the garden one Sunday afternoon and told him that she wanted to enter Carmel before Christmas of the same year. Both father and daughter broke down in floods of tears. Then Louis got up and gently picking a little white flower, with its root still intact, gave it to his daughter, talking to her about the care with which God had planted the flower and kept it until that day. Later, Thérèse wrote: 'I believed I was listening to my own story.' The flower seemed to Thérèse to be a representation of herself, 'destined to live in another soil'.

Thérèse was devoted to Eucharistic meditation and on 26 February, 1895, shortly before her passing, wrote what some have called her 'poetic masterpiece', '*To Live by Love*', which she had composed during Eucharistic meditation. During her remaining years, the poem was sent to various religious communities and included in a manuscript of her poems.

One of the most popular of the Christian saints, alongside St Francis, she is known and venerated by Christians and non-Christians alike around the world. The Basilica of Lisieux was consecrated on 11 July 1954 and is the second most visited place of pilgrimage after Lourdes in France, seating no fewer than 3000 people.

When the late Michael Hollings introduced and edited this little booklet in the *Enfolded in Love* series, he used the translation made many years ago by T.N. Taylor. Although Taylor's work has, in some respects, been superseded by others – notably John Clarke OCD – I have kept his translation, as fresh now, as it was over seventy years ago.

Luke Penkett, ObJN, CJN
The Julian Centre, Norwich

Seeking God's Will Humbly

When I say I am indifferent to praise, I do not mean the love and confidence shown me, which really touch my heart. But I feel that I have nothing now to fear from praise, and can listen to it unmoved, attributing to God all that is good in me. If it pleases him to make me appear better than I am, that does not concern me. He can act as he will.

My God, by how many different ways you lead souls! We read of saints who have left nothing behind them at their death, not a single written line. Others like St Teresa have enriched the Church with their teaching, not hesitating to reveal 'the secrets of the King', that he may the better be known and loved. Which of these two ways is more pleasing to God? It seems to me they are equally agreeable to him.

All those well loved by God have followed the inspiration of the Holy Spirit who commanded the prophet to write: 'Tell the just man that all is well' (Isaiah 3:10). Yes, all is well when we seek only the Master's will. So I obey Jesus when I try to obey his representative on earth.

Desire for Sanctity

I have always desired to become a saint, but in comparing myself with the saints I have always felt that I am as far removed from them as a grain of sand, trampled underfoot by the passer-by, is from the mountain whose summit is lost in the clouds.

Instead of feeling discouraged by such reflections, I concluded that God would not inspire a wish which could not be realized, and that in spite of my littleness I might aim at being a saint. 'It is impossible', I said, 'for me to become great, so I must bear with myself and my many imperfections.'

But I will seek out a means of reaching heaven by a little way – very short, very straight and entirely new. We live in an age of inventions. There are lifts which save us the trouble of climbing stairs.

I will try to find a lift by which I may be raised to God, for I am too small to climb the steep stairway of perfection.

Finding a Lift to God

I looked in Scripture to find some suggestion of what the lift I wanted might be. I came across these words from the book of Proverbs: 'Whoever is a little one, let that person come to me' (Proverbs 9:4). I therefore drew near to God, feeling sure I had discovered what I was looking for. But I wished to know more about what God would do to the 'little one'. So, I continued my search, and this is what I found: 'You shall be carried at the breasts and upon the knees: as one whom the mother caresses, so will I comfort you' (Isaiah 66: 12 – 13).

Never have I been consoled with more tender or sweet words. Jesus, your arms, then, are the lift which must raise me to heaven. To reach heaven I need not become great. On the contrary I must remain little. I must become even smaller than I am.

My God, you have gone beyond my desire and I will sing your mercies! 'You have taught me, Lord, from my youth, and I still declare your wonderful works, and shall do so till old age and grey hairs' (see Psalm 71: 17 – 18).

Wisdom – Old and Young

In this world, it is rare to find souls that do not measure God's omnipotence by their own narrow thoughts. The world is always ready to admit exceptions. Only God is denied that liberty.

I know it has long been the custom to measure experience by age – in his youth King David sang to the Lord: 'I am young and despised' (Psalm 119:141). But in the same psalm he does not fear to say: 'I have had understanding above old men, because I sought your commandments. Your word is a lamp to my feet and a light to my paths. I have sworn and I am determined to keep the judgements of your justice' (Psalm 119:100, 105, 106).

It was not thought imprudent to assure me once that the Lord was enlightening me and giving me the experience of years. I am now too little to be guilty of vanity, and too little to try to prove my humility by high-sounding words. I prefer, therefore, in all simplicity to own that 'He that is mighty has done great things to me' (Luke 1:49). The greatest of all is that he has shown me my littleness and how, of myself, I am incapable of anything good.

Trial of Darkness in Terminal Illness

When I returned to our cell in the evening of that happy day, I was still full of joy and I was quietly falling asleep, when, as on the previous night, Jesus gave me the same sign of my speedy entrance into eternal life.

My faith at this time was so clear and so lively that the thought of heaven was my great delight. I could not believe it possible that there were people without faith, and I was sure that those who deny the existence of another world belie their own convictions.

But during Easter, those days so full of light, the Lord made me understand that there are really souls bereft of all faith and hope. He allowed my own soul to be plunged into the thickest gloom. The thought of heaven which had been so sweet from my earliest years became for me a subject of torture.

The trial did not merely last for days or weeks. As I write, it has gone on for months and still I am waiting for relief. I wish I could explain what I feel, but it is beyond my power. One must have passed through the tunnel to understand how black its darkness is.

Sharing the Suffering of Unbelievers

I will suppose that I was born in a land of thick fog, that I had never seen nature in her smiling moods, or one single ray of sunshine. From my childhood I had heard of these things and knew that the country in which I lived was not my real home – that there was another land for which I must always long. This was no tall story invented by an inhabitant of the land of fogs. It was an unquestionable truth, for the king of that sunlit country had come to dwell for thirty-three years in the land of darkness, even though sadly: 'The darkness did not understand that he was the Light of the world' (see John 1:5).

But, Jesus, I believe firmly that you are the Light. I ask pardon for unbelieving people and am willing to eat the bread of sorrow as long as you will it. For love of you, I will sit at that table of bitterness where poor unbelievers take their food, and I will not rise from it till you give the sign. May I not say in my own name and in the name of unbelieving people: 'O God, be merciful to us sinners'? (See Luke 18:13).

May all those on whom faith does not shine at last see the light! If it is necessary for one who loves you to purify the table of unbelief, I am willing to remain there alone to eat the bread of tears until you bring me to your kingdom of light. I ask only that I may never offend you.

Attacks on Faith

From my childhood, I had had the conviction that I should one day be released from this land of darkness. I believed it not only from what I heard, but also because the deepest longings of my heart assured me that there was in store for me another and most beautiful country, a lasting place to live.

I was like Christopher Columbus whose genius anticipated the discovery of the New World. But suddenly the fog that surrounds me finds its way into my very soul. It so blinds me that I can no longer picture my promised home … it has faded away.

When my heart, weary of the enveloping darkness, tries to find some rest and strength in the thought of an everlasting life to come, my anguish only increases. It seems to me that the darkness itself, borrowing the voice of the unbeliever, cries mockingly: 'You dream of a land of light, you believe the Creator of this wonder will be yours for ever, you think you will escape one day from the mists in which you now languish. Hope on! Hope on! It will give you not what you hope for, but a night darker still – the night of utter nothingness!'

Trials in Coping with Faith

This description of what I suffer is as far removed from reality as the painter's rough outline from the model he copies. But to write more might be to blaspheme … even now I may have said too much. May God forgive me! He knows how I try to live by faith, even though it affords me no consolation.

I have made more acts of faith during the past year than in all the rest of my life. Whenever my enemy provokes me to combat, I try to behave like a soldier. Aware that a duel is an act of cowardice, I turn my back and tell Jesus, my Saviour, that I am ready to shed my blood for him as a witness to my belief in heaven.

I tell him that if he will open heaven for eternity to poor unbelievers, I am content to sacrifice during my life all joyful thought of the home which awaits me. So, in spite of this trial which robs me of all sense of enjoyment, I can still say: 'You have given me, Lord, a delight in your doings' (Psalm 92:4). For is there greater joy than to suffer for your love, Lord? Even if by impossibility you were not aware of my affliction, I should still be happy to bear it in the hope that by my tears I might prevent or atone for one sin against faith.

The Night of the Soul

You may think that I am exaggerating the night of my soul. If one judged by the poems I have composed this year, it might seem that I have been inundated with consolation, that I am a child for whom the veil of faith is almost rent asunder … But it is not a veil … it is a wall which reaches to the very heavens, shutting out the starry sky.

When I sing in my verses of the happiness of heaven and of the eternal possession of God, I feel no joy. I sing out of what I wish to believe. Sometimes, I confess a feeble ray of sunshine penetrates my dark night and brings me a moment's relief, but after it has gone, the remembrance of it, instead of consoling me, makes the blackness seem denser still.

And yet I have never experienced more fully the sweetness and mercy of the Lord. He did not send this heavy cross when it would, I believe, have discouraged me, but chose a time when I was able to bear it. Now it does no more than deprive me of all natural satisfaction in my longing for heaven.

Facing an Early Death

It seems to me that nothing stands in the way of my going to heaven. I no longer have any great desires, beyond that of loving till I die of love. I am free, and I fear nothing, not even what I once dreaded more than anything else, a long illness which would make me a burden to the community.

Should it please God, I am quite content to have my sufferings of body and soul prolonged for years. I do not shrink from a long life: I do not refuse the battle. The Lord is the rock upon which I stand – 'who teaches my hands to fight, and my fingers to war. He is my protector and I have hoped in him' (Psalm 144:1 – 2).

I have never asked God to let me die young, but I have always thought that this favour will be granted me.

Very often, God is satisfied with our wish to labour for his glory, and how immense are my desires to do so.

On Counselling Others

In the abstract it seems easy to do good to souls, to make them love God more and to mould them to one's own ideas. But when we put our hands to the work, we quickly learn that, without God's help, it is as impossible to do them good as to bring back the sun once it has set.

Our own tastes, our own ideas must be put aside, and in absolute forgetfulness of self we must guide souls not by our way but along the particular path which the Lord himself indicates. The chief difficulty does not, however, lie here. What costs more than anything else is to be compelled to note their faults, their slight imperfections, and to wage war against them.

Happily for these souls, ever since I placed myself in the arms of Jesus I have been like a watchman on lookout for the enemy from the highest tower of a castle. Nothing escapes me. Indeed my clear-sightedness often gives me matter for surprise, and makes me think it quite excusable for the prophet Jonah to have fled before the face of the Lord rather than announce the ruin of Nineveh.

I prefer a thousand reproofs rather than to inflict one, yet it is necessary the task should cause me pain, for if I spoke only through natural impulse, the souls at fault would not understand that they were in the wrong.

Firm Guidance of Souls

I gained knowledge guiding others. I realized that all souls have more or less the same battles to fight, but no two souls are exactly the same. Each one must be dealt with differently. With some I humble myself, confessing my own struggles and defeats. But this means they have less difficulty in acknowledging their faults, being consoled by the discovery that I know their trials from my own experience.

In dealing with others, my only hope of success lies in being firm and in never going back on what I have said, since self-abasement would be mistaken for weakness.

The Lord has given me the grace never to fear the conflict, to do my duty no matter what the cost. More than once it has been said to me: 'If you want to do anything with me, you must treat me with gentleness, you will gain nothing by being severe.' But no one is a good judge in one's own case. During a painful operation a child would be sure to cry out and say that the remedy is worse than the disease. Yet how great will be the little one's delight when he find himself cured and able to run about and play. Souls soon recognize that a little bitterness is preferable to a surfeit of sweetness.

The Way of Growth for a Soul

The change which takes place in a soul from one day to another is sometimes really marvellous. 'You did well to be severe with me yesterday,' someone said to me. 'At first I was indignant, but after I thought it all over, I saw you were right. I left you thinking that all was at an end between us and determined to have nothing more to do with you. I knew, though, that the suggestion was a temptation and I felt you were praying for me. I grew calm, the light began to shine, and I have come back to hear all you have to say.'

Only too happy to follow my heart, I hastened to serve some food less bitter to the taste. But I soon discovered that I must not go too far. A single word can bring to the ground the edifice that cost so many tears. If I let fall a single word which seemed to soften the hard truths of the day before, I noticed the individual trying to take advantage of the opening.

Then I had recourse to prayer. I turned to the Virgin Mary, and Jesus was victorious. My whole strength lies in prayer and sacrifice; these are my invincible weapons, and experience has taught me that the heart is won by them rather than by words.

The Power of Prayer

The power of prayer is indeed wonderful. It is like a queen, who, having free access always to the king, can obtain whatever she asks. To secure a hearing, there is no need to recite set prayers composed for the occasion – were this the case, I should indeed deserve to be pitied.

Apart from the Office [the daily prayer of the Church] which is a daily joy, I do not have the courage to search through books for beautiful prayers. They are so numerous that it would only make my head ache. Unable either to say them all or to choose between them, I do as a child would who cannot read – I just say what I want to say to God, quite simply, and he never fails to understand.

For me, prayer is an uplifting of the heart, a glance towards heaven, a cry of gratitude and love in times of sorrow as well as joy. It is something noble, something supernatural, which expands the soul and unites it to God.

When my state of spiritual aridity is such that not a single good thought will come, I repeat very slowly the Our Father and the Hail Mary, which are enough to console me, and provide food for my soul.

The Opinion of Others – God's Purpose

I cannot say God makes me walk in the way of exterior humiliation; he is content with humbling me in my inmost soul. In the eyes of creatures, success crowns all my efforts – I seem to walk the dangerous path of honour. In this respect, I understand the design of God.

If I were looked upon as a useless member of the community, incapable and wanting in judgement, I would not be asked to help others. And so the Lord has thrown a veil over my shortcomings, interior and exterior. Sincere compliments come to me, but the remembrance of my weakness is so constantly present to me that there is no room for vanity.

However, I tire at times of this oversweet food and long for something other than praise. Then the Lord serves me a salad, well-flavoured and mixed with plenty of vinegar, and without oil. At the moment I least expect it, this salad is set before me.

Lifting the veil that hides my faults, God allows people to see me as I really am, and they tell me quite simply how I try them and what they dislike in me. Strangely, this salad pleases me and fills my soul with joy. How can something so contrary to nature afford joy? Had I not experienced it I would not have believed it possible.

Liking and Loving Others

I have noticed that is the holiest who are most loved; everyone seeks their company and is on the watch to do them a service without waiting to be asked. Holy people who can bear to be treated with a want of respect and attention find themselves surrounded by an atmosphere of love. St John of the Cross says: 'All good things have come to me since I no longer seek them for myself.'

Imperfect people, on the other hand, are left alone. They receive the measure of politeness, but their company is avoided for fear a word spoken will hurt their feelings. When I say imperfect people, I mean those who, being supersensitive or wanting in tact or refinement, make life unpleasant for others. Defects of this kind seem incurable.

From this I conclude that I ought to seek the companionship of those for whom I have a natural aversion. Frequently it needs only a word or a smile to impart fresh life in a despondent soul. But it is not just to bring consolation that I try to be kind. I wish to please the Lord's gospel precept: 'When you make a feast, call the poor, the maimed, the blind and the lame, and you will be blessed, because they have nothing with which to recompense you, and your Father who sees in secret will repay you' (see Luke 14:13 – 14).

An Example of Struggling to Love

Let me give an instance of my struggle to be loving. For a long time my place of meditation was near a sister who fidgeted incessantly, either with her rosary or with something else. Possibly I alone heard her because of my very sensitive ear, but I cannot tell you to what extent I was tried by the irritating noise.

There was a strong temptation to turn round and with one glance to silence the offender. Yet in my heart I knew I ought to bear with her patiently, for the love God, first of all, and also to avoid causing her pain. I therefore remained quiet, but the effort cost me so much that sometimes I was bathed in perspiration and my meditation consisted merely in the prayer of suffering.

Finally I sought a way of gaining peace in my inmost heart at least. So I tried to find pleasure in the most disagreeable noise. Instead of vainly attempting not to hear it, I set myself to listen attentively as though it were delightful music, and my meditation – which was not the prayer of 'quiet' – was passed in offering this music to the Lord.

You see I am a very little soul and can offer to God only very little things. I still miss the opportunity of welcoming these small sacrifices which bring so much peace, but I am not discouraged and I shall try to be more watchful in the future.

'Draw Me', and We Will Run

One day after Holy Communion, the Lord made me understand the words of Solomon: 'Draw me; we will run after you' (Song of Songs 1:4). Jesus, there is no need then to say: 'In drawing me, draw all the souls I love.' The words 'Draw me' suffice. I dare therefore to borrow your own words which you used on your last night as a traveller on earth: 'I have manifested your name to the men whom you have given me out of the world. They were yours and you gave them to me; and they have kept your word. Now they know that all which you have given me is from you, because the words you gave me I have given to them and they have received them … I pray for them … and not for them only do I pray, but for those also who through their word will believe in me … I have made known your name to them and will make it known, that the love with which you have loved me may be in them and I in them' (see John 17).

I would repeat your words before losing myself in your love. Perhaps I am very daring, but for a long time you have allowed me to be daring. You have said to me, as the father to the prodigal son: 'All I have is yours' (Luke 15:31). Therefore I may use your own words to draw down favours from your Father in heaven upon all the souls under my care.

Love Attracts Love

My God, you know I have always desired to love you alone. I seek no other glory. Your love has gone before me since I was a child. It has grown with my growth.

Love attracts love. But my love is not even a drop in the ocean. To love you as you love me, I must borrow your own love – it is the only way which will satisfy my desire. Jesus, it seems to me that you could not have overwhelmed a soul with more love than you have poured out on mine, and that is why I dare to ask you to love those you have given me, even as you love me.

If in heaven I find you love them more than you love me, I shall rejoice, because I acknowledge that their deserts are greater than mine. But on earth I cannot conceive of any love comparable to that with which you have favoured me, without any merit of my own.

More on 'Draw Me'

I have not fully explained my thoughts on: 'Draw me, and we will run.' The Lord has said: 'No one comes to me unless the Father who has sent me draws him' (John 6:44), and further on he tells us: 'Everyone who asks shall receive; he that seeks shall find; and the one who knocks shall have it opened to him' (Matthew 7:8). And again he adds: 'If you ask the Father anything in my name, he will give it to you' (John 16:23).

No doubt it was for this reason that, long before the birth of Jesus, the Holy Spirit inspired these prophetic words: 'Draw me – we will run.'

In asking to be drawn, we seek an intimate union with the object that has led our heart captive. If iron and fire were endowed with reason, and the iron could say 'Draw me', would this not prove its wish to be identified with the fire to the point of sharing its substance? Well, such precisely is my prayer.

I ask Jesus to draw me into the fire of his love, and to unite me so closely to himself that he may live and act in me. I feel the more the fire of love consumes my heart, the more frequently I shall cry 'Draw me!' and the more will those souls who come into contact with mine run swiftly.

The Lever of Prayer

We shall run together because souls that are on fire can never remain inactive. They may, like Mary Magdalene, sit at the feet of Jesus, listening to his words. Though appearing to give him nothing, they give him far more than Martha, who was 'troubled about many things' (Luke 10:41).

It is not, of course, Martha's work that the Lord blames, for his own Mother humbly devoted herself to the self-same duty, having to prepare the meals for the Holy Family. What he does blame is Martha's excessive solicitude.

The power of prayer has been understood by all the saints, and especially, perhaps, by those who have illumined the world with the light of Christ's teaching. Was it not in prayer that St Paul, St Augustine, St Thomas Aquinas, St John of the Cross, St Teresa and so many other friends of God acquired the wonderful knowledge which has enthralled the loftiest minds?

Give me a lever and a fulcrum on which to rest it,' said Archimedes, 'and I will lift the world.' What the scientist could not obtain, because his request had a merely material end without reference to God, the saints have obtained in all its fullness. God has given them a fulcrum to lean upon himself alone, and for a lever the prayer which inflames with the fire of love. Thus they have uplifted the world, and on earth will continue to raise it till the end of time.

Trust in God's Merciful Love

Since the Lord is in heaven I can only follow him by traces full of light and fragrance which he has left behind him. When I open the Gospels, I breathe the fragrance exhaled by the life of Jesus, and I know which way to run.

It is not to the highest place but to the lowest that I hasten. Leaving the Pharisee to go forward, I repeat with all confidence the humble prayer of the publican. Most of all I imitate the behaviour of Mary Magdalene, for her amazing – or, rather, loving – audacity which delighted the heart of Jesus, has cast its spell upon mine.

It is not because I have been reserved from serious sin that I lift up my heart to God in trust and in love. I am certain that even if I had on my conscience every imaginable crime, I should lose nothing of my confidence, but would throw myself, my heart broken with sorrow, into the arms of my Saviour.

I remember his love for the prodigal son, I have heard his words to Mary Magdalene, to the woman taken in adultery, to the woman of Samaria. No – there is no one who could frighten me, for I know too well what to believe concerning his mercy and his love.

Self-surrender to Love

Do not think I am overwhelmed with consolations. Far from it! My joy consists in being deprived of all joy here on earth. Jesus does not guide me openly; I neither see nor hear him. Nor is it through books that I learn, for I do not understand what I read. Yet at times I am consoled by some chance words, such as the following which I read after a meditation passed in utter dryness: the Lord said to St Margaret Mary: 'Here is the master I give you. He will teach you all that you should do. I wish to make you read in the Book of Life in which is contained the science of love.'

The science of love – these words re-echo in my soul. I wish for no other knowledge, and like the spouse in the Canticle of Canticles, 'having given up all the substance of my house for love, I reckon it as nothing' (Song of Songs 8:7). I understand clearly that through love alone can we become pleasing to God, and my sole ambition is to acquire it.

Jesus points out to me the only way which leads to Love's furnace – that way is self-surrender – it is the confidence of the little child who sleeps without fear in its father's arms. The Spirit of Love declares: 'To him that is little, mercy is granted' (Wisdom 6:7). In his name, too, the prophet Isaiah foretells how on the last day the Lord 'will feed his flock like a shepherd; he will gather together the lambs in his arms, and shall take them to his bosom' (Isaiah 40:11).

Thirsting for Love

Isaiah's inspired gaze penetrated the depth of eternity and caused him to cry out: 'Thus says the Lord: You shall be carried at the breasts and upon the knees they shall caress you. As one whom the mother caresses, so will I comfort you' (Isaiah 66:12 – 13). After such words, I can only be silent and weep for very love. If all weak and imperfect people like me felt as I do, none would despair of reaching the summit of the mountain of love, since Jesus does not look for deeds, but only for gratitude and self-surrender.

Does he not say: 'Offer to God the sacrifice of praise and thanksgiving' (Psalm 50:14)? This is all the Lord claims of us. He wants our love, he has no need of our works. He has no need to tell us if he is hungry, but on earth he begged a little water from the Samaritan woman. But when he said 'Give me a drink' (John 4:7) he, the Creator of the universe, was asking for the love of his creatures.

He thirsted indeed, but he thirsted for love. His thirst today is more intense than ever. Among the disciples of this world he meets nothing but indifference and ingratitude. And, alas, among his own how few are the hearts that surrender themselves without reserve to the infinite tenderness of his love.

God's Reassurance for a Soul

I will address myself to the Lord, for by doing so I shall be better able to set down my thoughts. You may find my expressions exaggerated, but I assure you there is no exaggeration whatsoever in my heart – there all is peace and calm.

Jesus, how tenderly and how gently you lead my soul! While dwelling on the mysterious dreams you sometimes send to those you favour, I thought such consolations were not meant for me, for in my soul it was always night, darkest night. Then I fell asleep amid the fury of the storm.

Just before dawn the next morning, I dreamt I was walking in a gallery and saw three Carmelite sisters coming towards me. One came to me and I recognized the foundress of Carmel in France. She greeted me affectionately. I asked her: 'Does the Lord want more from me than these poor little acts and desires that I offer him? Is he pleased with me?' She answered: 'God asks nothing more of you: he is pleased, very much pleased.' My heart was full of joy, and I woke up.
I cannot express the happiness which filled my soul. On waking, I realized that heaven does exist. This impression remains.

The Variety of Vocations

I ought to be content to be a daughter of Carmel and by union with you, Jesus, to be the mother of souls. Yet, other vocations make themselves felt. I would be a priest, an apostle, a martyr, a doctor of the Church. I would like to do heroic deeds. I would gladly die in defence of the Church.

The vocation of priesthood! With what love, Jesus, would I bear thee in my hands when my words brought you down from heaven! With what love, too, would I give you to the faithful! And yet with all my longing to be a priest, I admire and envy St Francis of Assisi and feel drawn to imitate him by refusing that great dignity. How do I reconcile these opposite desires?

Like the prophets and doctors, I would be a light to souls. I would travel the world over, to preach your name and raise on non-Christian soil the standard of the cross. One mission alone would not satisfy my longings. I would spread the gospel in all parts of the earth, even to the farthest isles. I would be a missionary, but not for a few years only. Were it possible I should wish to be one from the world's creation and to remain one till the end of time.

But my greatest of all desires is to win the martyr's crown. Martyrdom was the dream of my youth, and the dream has only grown more vivid in Carmel's narrow cell.

The More Excellent Way

One day my eyes lighted upon chapters twelve and thirteen in St Paul's first epistle to the Corinthians. I read that all cannot become apostles, prophets and doctors: that the Church is composed of different members; that the eye cannot be the hand.

The answer was clear, but it neither satisfied my longing nor brought me the peace I sought. Then, in the words of St John of the Cross, 'descending into the depths of my nothingness, I was so lifted up that I reached to my aim'. Without being discouraged I read on and found comfort in this counsel: 'Be zealous for the better gifts. And I will show you a yet more excellent way' (1 Corinthians 12:31). The apostle then explains how all the better gifts are nothing without love, and that love is the most excellent way of going in safety to God. At last I had found rest.

But as I meditated on the body of the Church, I could not recognize myself among any of its members described by St Paul, or was it, rather, that I wished to recognize myself in all? Love gave me the key to my vocation. I understood that since the Church is a body composed of different members, she has a heart – a heart on fire with love.

My Vocation Is Love

I saw that love alone imparts life to all the members, so that should love ever fail, apostles would no longer preach the gospel and martyrs would refuse to shed their blood. Finally, I realized that love includes every vocation, that love is all things, that love is eternal, reaching down through the ages and stretching to the utmost limits of the earth.

Beside myself with joy, I cried out: 'Jesus, my love, my vocation is found at last – my vocation is love!' I have found my place in the Church and this place, Jesus, you have given me yourself; in the heart of the Church, I will be love. In this way I will be all things and my wish will be fulfilled.

But why do I say 'beside myself with joy'? It is, rather, peace which has claimed me, the calm, quiet peace of the sailor as he catches sight of the beacon which lights him to port. The beacon of love.

I am only a weak and helpless child, but my very weakness makes me dare to offer myself, Jesus, as a victim to your love. In the old days, only pure and spotless victims of holocaust would be accepted by God, and his justice was appeased only by the most perfect sacrifices. Now the law of fear has given way to the law of love, and I have been chosen, though weak and imperfect, as love's victim.

Love Repaid by Love

'Love is repaid by love alone' (St John of the Cross). Well do I know it, Jesus. Therefore I have sought out and found a way to ease my heart by giving you love for love. 'Use the riches that make men unjust, to find yourselves friends who may receive you into everlasting dwellings' (Luke 16:9). This is the advice you gave to your disciples after complaining that 'the children of this world are wiser in their generation than the children of light' (Luke 16:8).

I was a child of the light, and I understood that my desire of being all things, and of embracing every vocation, were riches that might well make me unjust; so I employed them in the making of friends. Mindful of the prayer of Eliseus when he asked the prophet Elijah for his double spirit, I presented myself before the company of angels and saints and said to them: 'I am the least of all creatures, I know my worthlessness, but I also know that generous hearts love to do good. I ask you to adopt me as your child. All the glory you may help me to acquire will be yours. Hear my prayer. Obtain for me a double portion of your love of God.'

I dare not try to understand all that my prayer means. I should fear to be crushed by the weight of its audacity. That I am, Jesus, your child, is my only excuse, for children do not grasp the full meaning of their words.

A Child of the Church

I am a child of the Church. I do not ask for riches or glory, not even for the glory of heaven. My own glory will be the reflection of the Church's glory. But I ask for love. My one thought, Jesus, is to love you. Great deeds are forbidden me. I can neither preach the gospel nor shed my blood – but what does it matter? Others labour while I, a little child, stay close to you and love you for all those who are in the strife.

How shall I show my love, since love proves itself with deeds? I will sign the canticle of love by each word and look, each little daily sacrifice. I wish to make profit out of the smallest actions and do them all for love. For love's sake I wish to suffer and to rejoice. Should my roses be gathered from among thorns, I will sing, and the longer and sharper the thorns, the sweeter will be my song.

Of what avail to you are my roses and my songs? Yet I know my shower of petals and my songs of love from my heart will be pleasing to you. You will use them for the Church.

I love you, Jesus, and bear in mind the words of St John of the Cross. 'The least act of pure love is of more value than all others works put together.'

Questioning the Reality of Love

Does pure love really exist in my heart? Are my boundless desires mere dreams, mere folly? If they are, enlighten me, Jesus, because you know I am only seeking the truth. If my desires are too bold, deliver me from them, for they are the most grievous of all martyrdoms.

Yet I confess that should I fail to reach the heights to which my soul aspires, I shall have tasted more sweetness in my martyrdom than I shall taste in eternal bliss. Jesus, the mere desire of your love awakens such delight, what must it be to possess it and enjoy it for ever?

How can a soul so imperfect as mine aspire to the fullness of love? What is the key to this mystery? My only friend, why do you not reserve these infinite longings for lofty souls, for the eagles which soar in the heights? I am only a little unfledged bird. Yet the eagle's spirit is mine and notwithstanding my littleness I dare to gaze upon the divine Sun of Love.

I would like to fly as the eagle does, but I can only flutter my wings – it is beyond my feeble strength to soar.

Confidence in Darkness

What is to become of me? Must I die of sorrow because of my helplessness? Oh no! I will not even grieve. With daring confidence, and reckless of self, I will remain there till death, my gaze fixed upon the divine Sun. Nothing will make me afraid, neither wind nor rain. Should impenetrable clouds conceal from my eyes the Sun of Love, should it seem to me that beyond this life there is only darkness, this would be the hour of perfect joy, the hour in which to urge my confidence to its uttermost bounds.

Knowing that beyond the dark clouds my Sun is shining, I should never dare to change my place.

This far, my God, I understand your love for me. But you know how often I lose sight of what is my only care, and, straying from your side, allow my wings to become draggled in the muddy pools of the world. Then 'I cry like a young swallow' (Isaiah 38:14) and my cry tells you everything. Then you remember in your infinite mercy that 'you came not to call the just, but sinners' (see Matthew 9:13).

The Divine Eagle

If you remain deaf to the plaintive cries of this feeble creature, should you hide yourself, then I am content to remain numb with cold, my wings bedraggled – and once more I would rejoice.

I am happy to feel myself so small and frail in your presence and my heart is at peace … for I know that all the eagles of heaven have pity on me and that they guard and defend me, putting to flight the vulture-like temptations which would destroy me.

I do not fear these temptations because I am not destined to be their prey, but the prey of the Divine Eagle.

Eternal Word, Saviour! You are the Divine Eagle whom I love. You draw me. You came into this land of exile, willing to suffer and to die, in order to carry away every single soul and plunge it into the very heart of Trinity – love's eternal home.

You returned to your realm of light, and still remain hidden here to nourish us, in our vale of tears, with Holy Communion. Forgive me if I tell you that your love reaches even to madness. At the sight of such folly, surely you expect my own heart to leap up to you? My trust can know no bounds.

The Folly of Love

I know well that for your sake the saints have made themselves foolish – being 'eagles', they have done great things. Too little for such deeds, my folly lies in the hope that your love will accept me, and in my confidence that the angels and saints will help me to fly to you.

As long as you will it, I shall remain with my gaze fixed on you, for I long to be fascinated by your divine eyes, to be a prey to your love.

I am filled with the hope that one day you will swoop down upon me and bear me away to the source of all love … that you will plunge me into its glowing abyss.

Jesus, I want to tell all little souls of the wonder of your love. If by any chance you could find a soul weaker than mine, which would abandon itself in perfect trust to your infinite mercy, I feel you would take delight in loading it with still greater favours.

Where do these desires to make known the secrets of your love come from? You alone can have taught them to me. You alone can reveal them to others. I ask you to look upon a vast number of little souls; choose in this world a legion of little people worthy of your love.

When Suffering is Sweet

It has come to this, that I can no longer suffer because all suffering is sweet. Besides, it is a mistake to worry as to what trouble may be in store: it is like meddling with God's work. We who run in the way of love must never allow ourselves to be disturbed by anything.

If I did not simply suffer from one moment to another, it would be impossible for me to be patient; but I look only at the present moment; I forget the past, and I take good care not to forestall the future. When we yield to discouragement or despair it is usually because we give too much thought to the past and to the future.

Pray for me; often when I cry to heaven for help it is when I feel most abandoned. But I turn to God and his saints and thank them notwithstanding. I believe they want to see how far I shall trust them. But the words of Job have not entered my heart in vain: 'Even if God should kill me, I would still trust him' (see Job 13:15).

I admit it has taken a long time to arrive at this degree of self-abandonment; but I have reached it now, and it is the Lord himself who has brought me there.

The Changing Moods of Love

The Lord's will fills my heart to the brim, and if anything else is added it cannot penetrate to any depth, but like oil on the surface of water it glides easily across. If my heart were not already brimming over, if it needed to be filled with feelings of joy and sadness that follow each other so rapidly, then indeed it would be flooded by bitter sorrow; but these quick succeeding changes scarcely ruffle the surface of my soul, and in its depths there reigns a peace that nothing can disturb.

Were it not for this trial of faith, which it is impossible to understand, I think I should die of joy at the thought of soon leaving this world.

I desire neither death nor life. Were the Lord to offer me a choice, I would not choose. I will only what he wills, and I am pleased with whatever he does. I have no fear of the last struggle, or of any pain, however great, which my illness may bring. God has always been my help; he has led me by the hand since I was a child, and I count on him now. Even though suffering should reach its furthest limits, I am certain he will never forsake me.

Trials, Temptations and Peace

One night, I was filled with a terrible feeling of anguish. I was lost in darkness from which came the cry: 'Are you certain God loves you? Has he come to tell you himself? The opinion of a few creatures will not justify you in his sight.' These thoughts had long tortured me, when I received a kind note from my superior, reminding me of the special graces with which Jesus had favoured me.

Peace and calm revived my heart, but then I thought the writer was prompted simply by affection for me. I turned to the Gospels, opening them at random, and I lighted upon a passage which had escaped me until then: 'He whom God sends, speaks the words of God, for God does not give his Spirit by measure' (John 3:34). I fell asleep, consoled.

One night I felt the evil one beside me. I could not see him but I could feel him near; he torments me, holding me with a grip of iron that I may not find a scrap of comfort, and adding to my discomfort that I may be driven to despair.

I cannot pray. I can only look at the Virgin Mary. I can only say 'Jesus'.

Mission of Love

I have never given God anything but love and it is with love he will repay. After my death, I will let fall a shower of roses.

It is love which attracts me in heaven. To love and to be loved and to return to earth to win love for our love.

One evening I heard some music from a distant concert, and the thought came that soon I shall be listening to the sweet melodies of heaven. This thought, however, gave me only a moment's joy, for one hope alone makes my heart beat fast – the love I shall receive and the love I shall be able to give!

I feel that my mission is soon to begin – to make others love God as I love him … to teach souls my little way. I will spend my heaven doing good on earth. This is not impossible, for the angels in heaven watch over us. No, there can be no rest for me till the end of the world, till the angel shall have said 'Time is no more' (Revelation 10:6). Then I shall take my rest, then I shall be able to rejoice, because the number of the elect will be complete.

The Little Way

My little way is the way of spiritual childhood, the way of trust and absolute self-surrender.

I want to point out to souls the means I have always found so completely successful, to tell them there is only one thing to do here below – to offer the Lord the flowers of little sacrifices and win him by our caresses. This is how I have won him, and that is why I shall be made so welcome.

If I should misguide you by my little way of love, do not fear that I shall allow you to continue following it. I should very soon come back to earth and tell you to take another road. But if I do not return, then believe in the truth of these words: 'We can never have too much confidence in God who is so mighty and so merciful. As we hope in him, so shall we receive.'

In my little way everything is more ordinary, for all I do must likewise be within everyone's reach.

Proofs of God's Love

Outwardly I am laden with proof of God's love. Nevertheless I remain in the deepest gloom! I am suffering intensely and yet amid it all I am in a state of extraordinary peace. All my longings have been realized.

One evening, I was in a high fever and parched with thirst. The infirmarian put a hot-water bottle to my feet and tincture of iodine on my chest. While submitting to these remedies, I could not help saying to the Lord: 'Jesus, you see I am already burning, and they have already brought me more heat and more fire. If, instead, they had given me even half a glass of water, what comfort it would have been. Jesus, I am very thirsty. But I am glad to have this opportunity for resembling you more closely and so saving souls.'

The infirmarian left me. Usually I did not see her again until the next day. What was my surprise when she returned with a refreshing drink. 'It has struck me', she said, 'that you may be thirsty, so for the future I shall bring you this each evening.' I looked at her in astonishment, and when she had left I could not keep back my tears. How good God is!

Passing the Light

Some time ago I was watching the flicker, almost imperceptible, of a tiny night-light. One of the sisters came up, and having lit her own candle in the dying flame, passed it round to light the candles of the others. And the thought came to me: 'Who dares glory in their own good works? It needs but one faint spark to set the world on fire.'

We come in touch with burning and shining lights set high on the candlestick of the Church, and we think we are receiving from them grace and light. But from where do they borrow their fire?

Very possibly from the prayers of some devout and hidden soul whose inward shining is not apparent to human eyes – some soul of unrecognized virtue, and in her own sight of little worth: a dying flame!

What mysteries we shall one day see unveiled! I have often thought that perhaps I owe all the graces with which I am laden to some little soul whom I shall know only in heaven.

Love Shared in Heaven

It is God's will here below that we shall distribute to one another by prayer the treasures with which he has enriched us. This is in order that, when we reach our everlasting home, we may love one another with grateful hearts and with affection far beyond that which is present in the most perfect family circle on earth.

In heaven, there will be no looks of indifference, because all the saints owe so much to one another. No envious glances will be cast, because the happiness of each is the happiness of all.

With the doctors of the Church we shall be like doctors; with the martyrs like martyrs, with the virgins like virgins. Just as the members of one family are proud of each other, so without the least jealousy we shall take pride in our heavenly brothers and sisters.

When we see the glory of the great saints, and know that through the secret workings of providence we have helped them to attain it, our joy and happiness will perhaps be as intense as theirs. A shepherd boy may be the familiar friend of an apostle or a doctor of the Church; a little child may be in close intimacy with a patriarch … How I long to enter the kingdom of love!

Holiness and Imperfection

Up to the age of fourteen, I made no progress. I practised virtue without tasting its sweetness. I desired suffering, but did not think of making it my joy. That came later. My soul was like a tree, the flowers of which had scarcely opened when they fell.

Offer God the sacrifice of never gathering any fruit off your tree. If it is his will that throughout your life you should feel a repugnance for suffering and humiliation – if he allows the flowers you desire and goodwill to fall to the ground without any fruit appearing – do not worry. At the hour of death, in the twinkling of an eye, he will cause rich fruits to ripen on the tree of your soul.

If I am looked upon as holy, it is, perhaps, because I have never desired to be considered so. But it is better for you to be found imperfect. Here is your chance of merit. To believe oneself imperfect and others perfect – this is true happiness.

Should earthly creatures think you wanting in virtue, they rob you of nothing. You are none the poorer; it is they who lose. For is there anything more sweet than the inward joy of thinking well of our neighbour?

The Lord Is My Judge

Jesus, you never ask what is impossible. You know better than I do how frail and imperfect I am. You know I shall never love others as you have loved them, unless you love them yourself within me. It is because you desire to grant me this grace, that you give a new commandment. I cherish it dearly, since it proves to me that it is your will to love in me all those you tell me to love.

When I show love towards others, I know that it is Jesus who is acting within me. The more closely I am united to him, the more dearly I love others. Should I wish to increase this love, and am put off by the defects of another person, I immediately try to look for that person's virtues and good motives. I call to mind that though I may have seen one fall, many victories over self may have been gained but have been concealed through humility. It can also be true that what appears to be a fault may very well be an act of virtue, because it was prompted by an act of virtue.

I have less difficulty in persuading myself that this is so, because of my own experience. Since my small acts of virtue can be mistaken for imperfection, why should not an imperfection be taken for a virtue? Since the Lord is my judge, I will try always to think leniently of others, that he may judge me leniently – or not at all, since he says 'Judge not and you will not be judged' (Luke 6:37).

True Love of Our Neighbour

Now I know that true love consists in bearing all my neighbour's defects, in not being surprised by mistakes but by being encouraged by the smallest virtues.

Above all else, I learnt that love must not be shut up in the heart, for: 'No man lights a candle and puts it in a hidden place, nor under a bushel; but upon a candlestick so that they who come in may see the light' (Luke 11:33). This candle, it seems to me, represents the love which enlightens and gladdens not only those who are dearest to us but all those who are of the household.

In the old Law, when God told his people to love their neighbour as themselves, he had not yet come down upon earth; and knowing full well the human being's strong love of self, he could not ask anything greater. But when Jesus gave his apostles 'his own commandment' (John 15:12), he not only asked us to love our neighbour as ourselves, but would have us love even as he does, and as he will do until the end of time.

The Beauty of Obedience

My soul is at peace, for long ago I ceased to belong to myself. I have surrendered my whole being to the Lord, and he is free to do with me whatever he pleases. He awakened in me an attraction to a life of complete exile, and asked me if I would consent to drink of that chalice. Without hesitation I tried to grasp it, but he withdrew his hand and showed me that my consent was all that he desired.

How much disquiet we free ourselves from by the vow of obedience. The simple religious is happy since her one guide is the will of her superiors. She has no fear of being misled, even when her superiors appear to be mistaken. But if she once fails to consult the unerring compass, she may quickly go astray.

By permitting me to suffer these temptations against faith, the Lord has increased within me the spirit of faith – that spirit which makes me see him communicating his will through my superiors. In the community, the burden of obedience is made sweet and light. But I feel my attitude would remain unchanged and my affection would not grow less if I were treated with severity.

I should still see the will of God manifesting itself in yet another way for the good of my soul.

Suffering and Love

Through my own dearly loved sisters in the community, Jesus has offered me more than one bitter chalice. King David was right when he sang 'Behold how good and how pleasant it is for brethren to dwell together in unity' (Psalm 133:1).

But perfect union can only exist upon earth in the midst of sacrifice. In coming to Carmel, I clearly foresaw that the restraining of natural affection would offer scope for great suffering.

How can it be said that it is more perfect to separate ourselves from those who are bound to us by ties of blood? Are brothers to be blamed who fight side by side on the same battlefield, or who win the martyr's palm? It is true that they encourage one another, but it is also true that the martyrdom of each inflicts a martyrdom on all.

It is the same in religious life, which theologians call a martyrdom. Each heart given to God loses nothing of its natural affection; on the contrary that affection grows stronger by becoming purer and more spiritual. It is with this love that I love my sisters. I am glad to fight beside them for the glory of God, but I am quite ready to go to another battlefield should the Lord so will it.

There would be no need even for an order – a look, a sign would suffice.

Choosing the Lowest Place

The lowest place is the only spot on earth which is not open to envy. Here alone there is neither vanity nor affliction of spirit. Yes, 'the way of a man is not his own' (Jeremiah 10:23), and sometimes we find ourselves wishing for things that dazzle. When that happens, there is nothing for it but to take our stand among the imperfect and look upon ourselves as very little souls who, at every instant, need to be upheld by the goodness of God.

He reaches out his hand to us the very moment he sees us fully convinced of our nothingness, and hears us cry out 'My foot stumbles, but your mercy is my strength' (Psalm 94:18). Should we attempt great things, however, even under the pretext of zeal, he deserts us. So all we have to do is to humble ourselves, to bear with meekness our imperfections. Herein, for us, lies true holiness.

When we are guilty of a fault, we must never attribute it to some physical cause such as illness, or the weather. We must ascribe it to our own imperfections, without being discouraged. 'Occasions do not make a man frail, but show what he is' (*On the Imitation of Christ*).

Dying

'To him who is little, mercy is granted' (Wisdom 6:7). It is possible to remain little even in the most responsible position. Besides, is it not written that at the last day 'the Lord will rise and save the meek and lowly ones of the earth'? (See Psalm 75:10.) He does not say 'judge' but 'save'.

Jesus, even now when you add bodily pains to those of my soul, I cannot bring myself to say 'the anguish of death has encompassed me' (see Psalm 18:5). Rather, I cry out in my gratitude: 'I have gone down into the valley of the shadow of death, but I fear no evil, because you, O Lord, are with me' (see Psalm 23:4).

All I have written of my thirst for suffering is really true. I have no regret for having surrendered myself to love.

I feel that my soul has never sought anything but the truth … I have understood humility of heart.

Is this not the agony? … Very well, then … be it so. I do not wish to suffer less.

Oh … I love him … My God. I … love … you!

Trust in the Lord

The moment I began counselling and instructing the souls entrusted to me, I saw at a glance that the task was beyond my strength. Quickly taking refuge in the Lord's arms, I imitated those babies who, when frightened, hide their faces on their father's shoulder. 'You see, Lord,' I said, 'that I am too small to feed your little ones, but if, through me, you will give to each what is necessary and suitable, then fill my hands. Without leaving the shelter of your arms or even turning my head, I will distribute your treasures to the souls who come to me asking for food. When they find it to their liking, I shall know that it is not to me they owe it, but to you. If on the contrary they complain, finding fault with its bitterness, I shall not be disturbed. I will try to persuade them that it comes from you, and will take care to give it to them.'

The knowledge that it was impossible to do anything of myself greatly simplified my task. Confident that the rest would be given me over and above, the one aim of my interior life was to unite myself more and more closely with God.

My hope has never been deceived. Each time I needed food for the souls in my charge, I always found my hands filled. Had I acted otherwise and relied on my own strength, I should very soon have been forced to surrender.

God Sounds the Heart

I do not depreciate thoughts which bring us nearer to God, but I have long been of the opinion that we must guard against overestimating their worth. Even the highest inspirations are of no value without good works.

Other people may obtain profit from these insights, provided they are grateful to God for being allowed to share them. But if the one who has received light from God should take pride in his spiritual wealth and imitate the Pharisee, that person becomes like someone dying of starvation before a well-spread table, while the guests enjoy the richest fare and cast envious glances at the possessor of so many treasures.

God alone can sound the heart! How short-sighted his creatures can be! They find a soul whose lights surpass their own; they think the Lord loves them less. Yet when did he lose the right to use one of his children to provide others with the nourishment they need? That right was not lost in the days of Pharaoh. God said to him: 'Therefore have I raised you, that I may show my power in you, and my name may be spoken throughout the earth' (Exodus 9:16). Centuries have passed since these words were spoken by God, but his ways have remained unchanged – he has always chosen human agents to accomplish his work among souls.

Love One Another

This year I received a deeper insight into the precept of love. I had never before fathomed the words of the Lord, 'The second commandment is like the first: You shall love your neighbour as yourself' (Matthew 22:39). I had worked above all to love God, and it was in loving him that I discovered the hidden meaning of these other words: 'Not everyone who says to me, Lord, Lord! shall enter into the kingdom of heaven, but he that does the will of my Father' (see Matthew 7:21).

This 'will' the Lord showed me through the words of his new commandment addressed to his apostles at the Last Supper, when he told them to love one another as he had loved them (see John 13:34).

I set myself to find out how he had loved his apostles, and I saw that it was not through their natural qualities, seeing that they were only ignorant men whose minds dwelt mostly on worldly things. Yet he calls them his friends, his brethren. He wants to see them near him in the Kingdom of his Father.

To open to them this Kingdom, he wills to die on the cross, saying 'Greater love than this no man has, than that a man lays down his life for his friends' (John 15:13).

Love Your Neighbour

In the Gospel the Lord showed me clearly what his new commandment demands. I read in St Matthew: 'You have heard it said that you should love your neighbour and hate your enemy; but I say to you, love your enemies and pray for those who persecute you' (Matthew 43 – 44).

We all have our natural likes and dislikes. We may feel more drawn to one person and may be tempted to go a long way round to avoid meeting another. Well, the Lord tells me that the latter is the one I must love and pray for, even though the manner shown me leads me to believe that the person does not care for me. 'If you love those that love you, what thanks are due to you? For sinners also love those who love them' (Luke 6:32).

Nor is it enough to love. We must prove our love. We take a natural delight in pleasing friends, but that is not love; even sinners do the same.

Generosity in Giving

Elsewhere, the Lord teaches me: 'Give to everyone who asks you; and if anyone takes away your goods, do not ask for them back again' (Luke 6:30). To give when asked is less pleasant than to give spontaneously and of one's own accord. Again, if a thing is asked for in a courteous way, consent is easy; but if, unhappily, tactless words have been used, there is an inward rebellion unless we are perfect in loving.

We discover no end of excuses for refusing, and it is only after having made clear to the guilty person how rude was their behaviour, that we grant as a favour what is required, or render a slight service which takes perhaps half the time we have lost in setting forth the difficulties and our own imaginary rights.

If it is difficult to give to anyone who asks, it is still more difficult to let what belongs to us be taken away without asking to have it back. I say it is difficult, but I should rather say it seems to be so, for 'the yoke of the Lord is sweet and his burden light' (Matthew 11:30).

When we submit to that yoke, we at once feel its sweetness.

Poor in Spirit

Jesus does not wish me to reclaim what belongs to me. This ought to appear quite natural, since in reality I own nothing, and ought to rejoice when an occasion brings home to me the poverty to which I am solemnly vowed. Formerly I used to think myself detached from everything, but since the Lord's words have become clear to me, I see how imperfect I am.

When starting to paint, for instance, if I happen to find the brushes in confusion, or a ruler or a penknife is missing, I am sorely tempted to lose patience, and have strongly to resist the impulse to demand, and sharply demand, the articles I want.

I may, of course, ask for them, and if I do so humbly, I am not disobeying the Lord's command. On the contrary, I am like the poor who hold out their hands for the necessaries of life and are not surprised when they are refused, because no one owes them anything.

The truly poor in spirit ask with detachment for what is really needful: not only are they refused, but an attempt is made to deprive them of what they possess already. Yet they follow the Lord's advice: 'If any man takes away your coat, let your cloak go also' (Matthew 5:40).

Attachment

When the Lord tells me to give to anyone who asks of me, and to allow what is mine to be taken without asking for it back, it seems to me that he speaks not only of earthly things but also of the good things of heaven. Neither the one nor the other is really mine; I renounced the first by a vow of poverty and the others are gifts which are simply lent. If God withdraws them, I have no right to complain.

But our own ideas, the fruit of our mind and heart, we regard as a sacred and personal treasury upon which no one may lay hands. For instance, if I tell someone of a light given me in prayer and that person afterwards reveals it as though it had been given to them, it would seem that what is mine is being appropriated.

Had I not experienced these human weaknesses, I could not explain them so well. I should have preferred to believe myself the only one who endured such petty temptations, but I was told to be prepared to listen to others and give suitable advice when asked. So I have learnt much, and in giving advice I found myself forced to practise what I preached.

I can now say truthfully that by God's grace I am no more attached to the gifts of the intellect than I am to material things. Should a thought of mine please someone, I find it quite easy to let them regard it as their own.

The Lord Loves a Cheerful Giver

It seems to me that to give up one's cloak is to renounce every right and to look upon oneself as the servant of all. However, divested of your cloak it is easier to walk or run, so the Lord adds: 'Whoever forces you to go for one mile, go with him two' (Matthew 5:41). So, it is not enough for me to give to the one who asks. I ought to anticipate the wish. I should show myself honoured by the request for service. If anything set aside for use is taken away, I should appear to be glad to be rid of it.

I cannot always carry out the letter of the gospel, for occasions arise when I am compelled to refuse a request. Yet, when love has taken deep root in the soul, it shows itself outwardly, and there is always a way of refusing so graciously what one cannot give, that the refusal affords as much pleasure as the gift itself.

It is true that people are more ready to beg from those who are most ready to give. Still, on the pretext that I shall be forced to refuse, I ought not to avoid an importunate person, since the Lord said: 'From the one who would borrow from you do not turn away' (Matthew 5:42).

The Cost of the First Step

I should not be kind for the sake of being considered so, nor in the hope that the other person will return the service, for once again it is written: 'If you lend to them of whom you hope to receive, what credit is that to you? For sinners also lend to sinners to receive as much again. But you do good and lend, hoping for nothing in return, and your reward will be great' (Luke 6:34 – 35).

Along this path it is the first step which costs, and even on earth the reward will be great. To lend without hope of return may seem hard; one would rather give outright, for a thing once given is no longer ours. When a person comes and says 'May I borrow your help for a few hours, and you may rest assured that later on I will do as much for you,' we may be practically certain that the time so lent will never be repaid, and therefore we feel sorely tempted to say 'I will *give* you what you ask!' The remark would gratify self-love, it being more generous to give than to lend, and in addition it would let the person feel how little reliance you put in their promise.

The divine precepts certainly run counter to our natural inclinations, and without the help of grace it would be impossible to understand them, far less to put them into practice.

Love Covers the Multitude of Sins

It may be that at some future day my present state will appear to me full of defects, but nothing now surprises me. Nor does my utter helplessness distress me. I even glory in it, and expect each day to reveal some fresh imperfection. Indeed, these lights on my own nothingness do me more good than lights on matters of faith.

Remembering that 'love covers the multitude of sins' (Proverbs 10:12), I draw from the rich mine which Jesus has opened up for us in the Gospels. I search the depth of his words and cry out with the Psalmist: 'I have run in the way of your commandments since you have enlarged my heart' (Psalm 119:32).

Only love can enlarge my heart. Jesus, ever since the flame of love consumes me, I run with delight in the way of your new commandment, and I desire to run until that glorious day when I follow you to your Kingdom, singing the canticle of love.

God in his goodness has given me a clear insight into the deep mysteries of love. If only I could express what I know, you would hear heavenly music; but I can only stammer like a child, and if the words of Jesus were not my support, I would be tempted to hold my peace.

Bibliography

Since 1973, two centenary editions of Thérèse's original, unedited manuscripts, including *The Story of a Soul*, her letters, poems, prayers and the plays she wrote for the Carmel recreations have been published in French. ICS Publications has issued a complete critical edition of her writings: *Story of a Soul*, *Last Conversations*, and the two volumes of her letters were translated by John Clarke, O.C.D.; *The Poetry of Saint Thérèse* by Donald Kinney, O.C.D.; *The Prayers of St Thérèse* by Alethea Kane, O.C.D.; and *The Religious Plays of St Thérèse of Lisieux* by David Dwyer and Susan Conroy. There are many translations of Sr Thérèse's autobiography under a wide variety of different titles:

Saint Thérèse of Lisieux, *The Story of a Soul,* translated by Thomas N. Taylor, Burns & Oates, 1944

Saint Thérèse of Lisieux, *Story of a Soul: the Autobiography of St Thérèse of Lisieux,* translated by John Clarke, O.C.D. (3rd ed.), Institute of Carmelite Studies Publications, 1996

Pierre Descouvemont, *Thérèse and Lisieux*, Novalis Publishing, 2003

Guy Gaucher, *Story of a Life: St Thérèse of Lisieux,* Harper Collins, 1993

Ida Friederike Gorres, *The Hidden Face: A Study of St Thérèse of Lisieux* (8th ed.), Pantheon, 1959

Vernon Johnson, *Spiritual Childhood: The Spirituality of St Thérèse of Lisieux* (3rd ed.), Ignatius Press, 2001

Ann LaForest, *Thérèse of Lisieux: the way to love,* Rowman & Littlefield, 2000

Joan Monahan, *St Therese of Lisieux: Missionary of Love*, Paulist, 2003

Thomas R. Nevin, *Thérèse of Lisieux: God's gentle warrior,* Oxford University Press, 2006

Patricia O'Connor, *Thérèse of Lisieux: a biography,* Our Sunday Visitor Press, 1983

Further reading

Thomas Keating, *St Thérèse of Lisieux: a transformation in Christ,* Lantern Books, 2001

Murchadh O'Madagain, *Thérèse of Lisieux: Through Love and Suffering,* Saint Paul Publications, 2003

Constant Tonnelier, *15 Days of Prayer with Saint Thérèse of Lisieux*, New City Press, 2011

Index

Page of Readings	Page in Taylor
15	151
16	151
17	152
18	153
19	155
20	155
21	156
22	157
23	157
24	158
25	176
26	177
27	178
28	179
29	181
30	182
31	186
32	190
33	192
34	193
35	193
36	194
37	196
38	197
39	198
40	201

41	202
42	203
43	204
44	205
45	206
46	207
47	207
48	208
49	222
50	222
51	223
52	230
53	232
54	234
55	301
56	301
57	299
58	163
59	162
60	160
61	158
62	302
63	236
64	175
65	171
66	162
67	164
68	165
69	165
70	170
71	166
72	167
73	170